MEET MARTIN LUTHER KING JR.

MELODY S. MIS

PowerKiDS press.

New York

To Roberta and Otis Parkman

Published in 2008 by The Rosen Publishing Group, Inc.
29 East 21st Street, New York, NY 10010

First Edition

Editors: Nicole Pristash and Jennifer Way
Book Design: Julio Gil
Photo Researcher: Nicole Pristash

Photo Credits: Cover © Time & Life Pictures/Getty Images; back cover, title page, headers, pp. 5, 7, 15, 17, 19 © Getty Images; pp. 9, 11, 13, 21 © Associated Press.

Library of Congress Cataloging-in-Publication Data

Mis, Melody S.
  Meet Martin Luther King Jr. / by Melody S. Mis. — 1st ed.
     p. cm. — (Civil rights leaders)
  Includes bibliographical references and index.
  ISBN 978-1-4042-4209-8 (library binding)
  1. King, Martin Luther, Jr., 1929–1968—Juvenile literature. 2. African American civil rights workers—Biography—Juvenile literature. 3. Civil rights workers—United States—Biography—Juvenile literature. 4. Baptists—United States—Clergy—Biography—Juvenile literature. 5. African Americans—Biography—Juvenile literature. 6. African Americans—Civil rights—History—20th century—Juvenile literature. 7. Civil rights movements—United States—History—20th century—Juvenile literature. I. Title.
  E185.97.K5M56 2008
  323.092—dc22
  [B]
                                        2007034839

Manufactured in the United States of America

Contents

Meet Martin Luther King Jr.   4

Segregation   6

Life in the North   8

Working for Civil Rights   10

The SCLC   12

Peaceful Protests   14

"I Have a Dream"   16

The Right to Vote   18

The Chicago Freedom Movement   20

Honoring Martin Luther King Jr.   22

Glossary   23

Index   24

Web Sites   24

"I have a dream." These are the words Martin Luther King Jr. spoke at a **rally** in Washington, D.C., in 1963. King's dream was that all people would be treated equally. He hoped that people of all races would learn to live together in peace.

At that time, African Americans in the South did not have the same civil rights as white people had. Civil rights are the rights that all citizens have. King believed this was wrong. He spent his life working for equality and civil rights. He became one of our nation's great leaders. His life and his work are still honored today.

Martin Luther King Jr. did not blame one group of people for the inequalities that blacks faced. He felt each person should work for world peace and equality.

Martin Luther King Jr. was born in Atlanta, Georgia, on January 15, 1929. As a child, King was a good student. He finished high school at 15 and then went on to Morehouse College, in Atlanta. From there, he went to schools in Pennsylvania and Massachusetts, where he studied to be a **minister**.

From early on in his life, King learned that people could be cruel. He was treated badly by some white people because he was black. This was because of segregation. Segregation means that black people were kept apart from white people. King did not understand why his color should matter. He decided to work hard toward ending segregation.

At age six, Martin made friends with some white children. One day, he went to their house to play. The friends' mother would not let her children play with Martin because he was black.

Segregation meant that African Americans had to go to different public places than white people. Blacks could not go to white schools or live where whites lived.

7

When King went to Boston University, he met Coretta Scott. She was studying to be a singer. They married on June 18, 1953.

The Kings liked living in the North because they had more **freedom** there. They could go out with their white friends whom they knew from school. They could eat at any **restaurant**. They could sit wherever they wanted to in **theaters** and buses.

King finished his studies at Boston University in 1954. Northern and southern churches wanted him to be their minister. King picked the Dexter Avenue Baptist Church in Montgomery, Alabama. He wanted to work for civil rights in the South.

Coretta Scott King helped her husband with his civil rights work. She was often right by his side at rallies and during his successes.

In 1955, King helped start the civil rights **movement**. It began in Montgomery, Alabama. An African-American woman named Rosa Parks refused to give up her seat to a white person on a public bus. She was caught and put in **jail**.

King believed African Americans should stand up for their rights. In college, he had read about peaceful **protests**. After Parks's **arrest**, King led a peaceful bus **boycott**. African Americans stopped riding the public buses for a year. During the boycott, King was arrested. Finally, the government said that Alabama could not segregate its buses. King's ideas were working.

During this meeting on December 5, 1955, King asked the black people of Montgomery to stop riding the city's buses. This marked the beginning of the Montgomery Bus Boycott.

The SCLC

In 1957, Martin Luther King and other black ministers formed the SCLC, or the Southern Christian Leadership Conference. The SCLC wanted to get people to protest against segregation. Many white people helped African Americans with Freedom Rides and sit-ins as well.

During sit-ins, the protesters would go to restaurants that did not allow African Americans and order food. The restaurant would not serve them. Sometimes, the protesters were arrested if they would not leave. King was often put in jail during these protests. The SCLC helped people see that **discrimination** is wrong.

Whites and African Americans would travel on buses in the South and sit in the seats saved for white people. When the buses stopped at restaurants, the protesters held sit-ins. These were called Freedom Rides.

On October 19, 1960, these protesters held a sit-in to protest segregation at a store in Atlanta, Georgia. It was one of the first sit-ins of the civil rights movement.

King believed peaceful protests were the best way to make others see the problems African Americans faced. He was right.

In 1963, King and the SCLC planned a protest march in Birmingham, Alabama. The protest was against businesses that would not hire or sell their goods to African Americans. On May 2, 1963, more than 2,500 schoolchildren peacefully marched through downtown Birmingham. The police sprayed the children with water to get them to move. The public became angry when they saw this on TV. Birmingham businesses were forced to stop segregating. King's hope that peaceful protests would work was coming true.

Large groups of people took part in peaceful protests during the civil rights movement. They held signs, sang songs, and talked about how to gain peace.

In August 1963, Martin Luther King Jr. led the March for Jobs and Freedom in Washington, D.C. The march was the largest rally ever held in the city. More than 250,000 people from all over the country gathered for the march.

During the march, people sang songs and gave speeches. King talked about his dream of equality and peace. He wanted to end segregation in schools. He also wanted to stop discrimination in the workplace. His speech was powerful. He was asked to help write a law that would guarantee, or promise, equal rights for African Americans. This became the Civil Rights Act that the government passed in 1964.

Martin Luther King Jr.'s famous "I have a dream" speech was an important moment in U.S. history. His words are still remembered and spoken today.

King's speeches and peaceful marches for civil rights were successful. The South stopped segregation in its schools and public places.

One problem remained, though. Whites would not let black people vote in **elections**. This caused King to plan marches from Selma to Montgomery, Alabama. During the marches, three blacks were killed and many were beaten. This made Americans angry. They pressed the government to pass the Voting Rights Act of 1965.
Under this act, the government watched over elections to make sure that blacks could vote.

In 1964, King received the Nobel Peace Prize for his work in civil rights. The Nobel Peace Prize is given to people who work very hard toward spreading peace.

Martin Luther King Jr. received the Nobel Peace Prize on December 10, 1964. He was the youngest man ever to receive this prize.

In 1966, Martin Luther King Jr. decided to take his peaceful protests to Chicago, Illinois. He picked Chicago because many African Americans lived in bad **conditions** there. He found that many people would not sell or rent houses to black people. King wanted to stop this discrimination.

Even though some people said they would kill him, King went on with his marches. He wanted the protests to be peaceful, but many turned bad. White people threw things at the protesters. When King left Chicago, he put a student named Jesse Jackson in charge of the Chicago Freedom Movement.

Martin Luther King Jr. helped clean up bad neighborhoods in Chicago, where many blacks lived. Here, King (far right) is helping rebuild a building that was in bad shape.

Martin Luther King Jr. continued his fight over the next few years. Sadly, his fight ended too soon. On April 4, 1968, King was in Memphis, Tennessee, planning a march. While he was talking to friends at his motel, he was shot and killed. People of all races were sad about his death.

King showed the nation that peaceful protests could make changes. He worked for equal rights for all people and he succeeded. He was given many honors for his work, such as the Presidential Medal of Freedom. Martin Luther King Jr. is one of America's most important leaders. Every year, Americans honor his life on the third Monday in January.

Glossary

arrest (uh-REST) Stopping a person who is thought to have done a crime.

boycott (BOY-kot) Refusing to buy from or deal with a business.

conditions (kun-DIH-shunz) The ways people or things are or the shape they are in.

discrimination (dis-krih-muh-NAY-shun) Treating a person badly because he or she is different.

elections (ee-LEK-shunz) Picking someone for a position by voting for him or her.

freedom (FREE-dum) The state of being free.

jail (JAYL) A building where people who do a crime are locked up.

minister (MIH-nuh-ster) A person who leads services in a church.

movement (MOOV-ment) A group of people who get together to back the same cause.

protests (PROH-tests) Acts of disagreement.

rally (RA-lee) A gathering of people to back something.

restaurant (RES-tuh-rahnt) A place where food is made and served.

theaters (THEE-uh-turz) Buildings where plays and movies are shown.

Index

A

Alabama, 8, 10, 14, 18

B

Boston University, 8

C

Civil Rights Act, 16

F

Freedom Rides, 12

J

Jackson, Jesse, 20

K

King, Coretta Scott (wife), 8

M

March for Jobs and
    Freedom, 16
Memphis, Tennessee, 22

P

Parks, Rosa, 10
Presidential Medal of
    Freedom, 22
protest(s), 10, 12, 14, 20,
    22

R

rally, 4, 16

S

segregation, 6, 12, 16, 18
sit-in(s), 12
Southern Christian
    Leadership Conference
    (SCLC), 12, 14

Web Sites

Due to the changing nature of Internet links, PowerKids Press has developed an online list of Web sites related to the subject of this book. This site is updated regularly. Please use this link to access the list:
www.powerkidslinks.com/crl/mlk/

4/12 (12)
1/15 (18)